Macroeconomic indicators and ind

Economic objectives are measured through a number of official indicators. Major macroeconomic indicators include:

- gross domestic product
- the inflation rate
- the unemployment rate
- the budget balance
- the balance on th
  payments

Macroeconomic indicators are usually expressed in numerical values or rates. Index numbers are a useful way of presenting time-series data or data for multiple indicators presented together for the purpose of comparisons.

---

⑫ **Define the term 'GDP per capita'. (AO1)** `3 marks`

⑬ **Define the term 'unemployment rate'. (AO1)** `3 marks`

⑭ **Distinguish between real and nominal GDP. (AO1)** `3 marks`

⑮ **In an economy the CPI was 209 in February 2016. If in February 2015 the CPI had been 203, calculate the inflation rate for the year to February 2016. (AO1, AO2)** `4 marks`

⑯ **Explain two reasons why the labour force survey measure of unemployment will be different from that of the claimant count measure. (AO1, AO2)** `4 marks`

⑰ **Explain two features of the CPI as used to calculate UK inflation. (AO1, AO2)** `6 marks`

18 The following data relate to an economy.

Year	Nominal GDP (in $bn)	Price level
2015	1,600	142
2016	1,675	146

a Calculate the level of real GDP in 2016. (AO1, AO2) 4 marks

....

....

b Calculate the level of economic growth in real terms between 2015 and 2016. (AO1, AO2) 4 marks

....

....

....

19 The following data relate to a small economy.

Year	Nominal GDP (in £m)	Price level
2015	2,460	104
2016	2,504	109

a Calculate the level of real GDP in 2016. (AO1, AO2) 4 marks

....

....

b Calculate the inflation rate for the year 2016. (AO1, AO2) 4 marks

....

....

c Calculate the level of economic growth in real terms between 2015 and 2016. (AO1, AO2) 4 marks

....

....

20 Group the following into (i) macroeconomic objectives and (ii) macroeconomic indicators. (AO1) 6 marks

a Low unemployment

b Claimant count unemployment

c Labour force survey unemployment

d Low changes in CPI

e Current account of the balance of payments

f Stable and consistent increases in GDP

....

....

21 Consider the following statement: 'The average level of price increases is lower this year than in previous years but inflation is still above target.'

In the light of the above statement, decide whether the following statements are true or false: (AO1)

`4 marks`

a The economy is now experiencing deflation.

b Inflation is lower now than it was last year.

c Goods and services are now cheaper than in the previous year.

d The government has yet to achieve its inflation target.

22 Explain why the population may receive higher real incomes despite a fall in the rate of economic growth. (AO1, AO3)

`3 marks`

23 An index number for an economic variable is as follows:

Year 1	100
Year 2	150
Year 3	200

Based on the above table, decide which of the following statements are true and which are false. (AO1)

`2 marks`

a By year 3, the variable has doubled in size compared with the start.

b There was a 50% increase in the variable between year 1 and year 2.

c The variable grew equally fast in year 2 as it did in year 3.

d There was a 50% increase in the variable between year 2 and year 3.

24 Study the following extract, table and graph and answer the questions that follow.

UK GDP finally surpasses its pre-recession peak

In summer 2014, UK GDP was calculated to have finally overtaken the level previously achieved in early 2008. GDP has actually been increasing since mid-2009 but, given the speed of the recovery, only recovered the lost ground around 5 years after the end of the recession. Annual growth in 2014 was 3%, which was encouraging for a government that had looked like it would not gain re-election in 2015.

If growth was lower than expected in the immediate aftermath of the recession, one surprise was the fall in unemployment that followed the end of the recession. Normally unemployment is a lagging variable which can often only follow changes in GDP after a period of over 1 year, as firms are often cautious about hiring new workers once economic growth resumes.

Year	Economic growth (% change)
2000	3.8
2001	2.7
2002	2.5
2003	4.3
2004	2.5
2005	2.8
2006	3.0
2007	2.6
2008	−0.3
2009	−4.3
2010	1.9
2011	1.6
2012	0.7
2013	1.7
2014	3.0

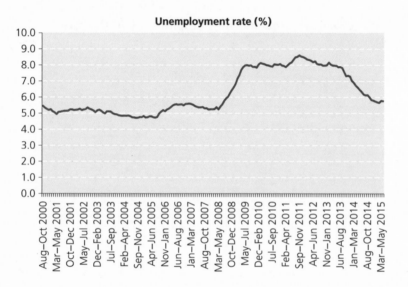

a In which year between 2000 and 2014 was economic growth: (AO1)   `2 marks`

   i Highest?

   ii Lowest?

   ....

   ....

b Is there a policy conflict in achieving economic growth and reducing unemployment? Use the data to support your reasoning. (AO1, AO2)   `4 marks`

   ....

   ....

   ....

   ....

   ....

   ....

   ....

c Using the data on page 8, identify two significant points of comparison between the unemployment rate and the rate of economic growth between 2000 and 2014. (AO1, AO2)

4 marks

....

....

....

....

....

d Explain three reasons why a government would be keen to see economic growth rising. (AO1, AO2)

6 marks

....

....

....

....

....

....

....

....

8

Exam-style questions: multiple choice

Circle the letter of the answer that you think is correct.

25 The following table shows real GDP for an economy expressed in the form of index numbers with 2010 as the base year.

Year	Real GDP 2010 = 100
2010	100
2011	99
2012	101
2013	104
2014	107

Which of the following statements is true for this economy?

A Economic growth was fastest between 2013 and 2014

B The economy was probably in recession between 2011 and 2012

C Economic growth between 2012 and 2013 was 3%

D Economic growth was fastest between 2012 and 2013

26 The table below shows nominal GDP expressed as an index number and the price level index (CPI) for an economy for 2014 and 2015.

	2014	2015
GDP	150	160
CPI	140	148

Which of the following statements is *not* true, based on these data? 1 mark

A   Inflation for the period was over 5%

B   Real GDP rose for the economy

C   Per capita income rose in nominal and real terms

D   Nominal economic growth was over 5%

27 Which of the following is a macroeconomic objective of the government? 1 mark

A   Minimising economic growth

B   High but stable budget deficit

C   Stable prices

D   Rising current account deficit

28 Government spending in excess of taxation revenue is commonly known as a: 1 mark

A   Trade deficit

B   Budget deficit

C   Balance of payments deficit

D   Current account deficit

29 Consider the following data relating to the price index for an economy.

	Price index
2012	100
2013	98
2014	103
2015	104

Which of the following statements is true, based on these data? 1 mark

A   Inflation was highest in 2015

B   The economy experienced deflation in 2013

C   Money gained in value over the period 2012–14

D   All prices rose over the period 2012–14

Exam-style questions: data response

30 ⏱ 30

30 Read Extracts A, B and C and answer the following questions. **25 marks**

Extract A

The consumer prices index (CPI) between July 2014 and July 2015

	CPI
July 2014	127.8
Aug 2014	128.3
Sep 2014	128.4
Oct 2014	128.5
Nov 2014	128.2
Dec 2014	128.2
Jan 2015	127.1
Feb 2015	127.4
Mar 2015	127.6
Apr 2015	128.0
May 2015	128.2
Jun 2015	128.2
July 2015	128.0

Extract B

The inflation rates based on both the CPI and the retail price index (RPI) for 2014 to 2015

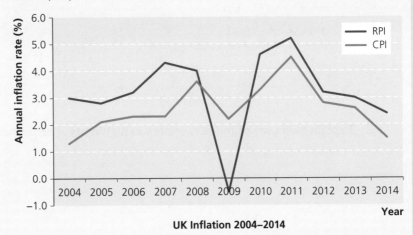

UK Inflation 2004–2014

Extract C

The inflation 'basket' has recently been updated. To ensure this basket provides a representative sample of goods purchased by the typical UK household, it has to be updated on an annual basis — bringing in goods which are either new to the market or being purchased in greater quantities than before. Additions to the 2015 basket include e-cigarettes, whereas items removed from the basket include Satnavs (most new cars have them already installed). Ironically, the fear of policy makers in 2015 comes not from inflation but rather from deflation.

a **Define the term 'deflation'.** **3 marks**

....

....

....

b **Using Extract A, calculate the inflation rate for the year to July 2015.** **4 marks**

....

....

....

....

....

....

....

c Using Extract B, identify two significant points of comparison between the
   RPI inflation rate and the CPI inflation rate over the period 2004 to 2014.

4 marks

d Explain two uses of index numbers in highlighting economic data.

4 marks

e Explain the limitations of using the CPI data to represent the inflation rate
   experienced by households.

10 marks

Topic 2

How the macroeconomy works

National income and the circular flow of income

National income represents the income for the whole economy. This statistic is usually represented by the gross domestic product (GDP) of the economy.

An economic model shows us a simple representation of how the macroeconomy actually works. One such model is the circular flow of income. This model shows us how real national income is determined and how national income will rise or fall depending on the actions of households and businesses, and — in a more complex model of the circular flow — how the government sector and the foreign trade sector influence the level of national income.

1 Define the term 'circular flow of income'. (AO1) **3 marks**

....

....

2 Define the term 'macroeconomic equilibrium'. (AO1) **3 marks**

....

....

3 Explain why including both the output of a logging company which sells felled trees and the output of a pine furniture retailer in the national income accounts is likely to be a mistake. (AO1, AO2) **3 marks**

....

....

....

4 Explain two uses of national income data by the government. (AO1, AO2) **4 marks**

....

....

....

....

5 Explain why the income method and the expenditure method should always give the same total for the GDP of an economy and then explain why in reality they are rarely the same. (AO1, AO2) **4 marks**

....

....

....

....

6 Give three examples each of (i) injections and (ii) withdrawals. (AO1) 6 marks

7 The government in an economy with a balanced budget has a deficit on the current account of £5 billion. If the level of investment in the economy is £25 billion, calculate the level of savings needed to bring the macroeconomy into equilibrium. (AO1, AO2) 4 marks

8 The following data relate to an economy.

	£ billion
Investment	75
Saving	50
Imports	45
Government spending	100
Taxation	90

If this economy is in macroeconomic equilibrium, calculate the level of exports. (AO1, AO2) 4 marks

9 Assuming the economy is in equilibrium in each scenario, complete the following table. (AO1, AO2) 4 marks

	Investment (£m)	Saving (£m)	Taxation (£m)	Government spending (£m)	Exports (£m)	Imports (£m)
Scenario 1		313,123	363,634	424,231	12,123	304,938
Scenario 2	2,413,432	4,101,810		7,356,452	344,241	567,003
Scenario 3	39,080	41,511	65,446	123,131		187,566
Scenario 4	222,678	231,707	602,080		765,654	698,080

Space for workings

10 The following table contains estimates of the GDP of a range of countries for 2014 as well as an estimate of their population level for 2015.

	Population (2015 estimate) (millions)	GDP (PPP*) (2014 estimate) ($ billions)
China	1,370	17,600
India	1,276	7,400
USA	322	17,400
New Zealand	4.6	159

*PPP refers to purchasing power parity — this is a specific rate of exchange between currencies used to make comparisons of monetary value more representative of the purchasing power of money in that economy.

a For each country, calculate the GDP per capita. (AO1, AO2) **8 marks**

b If economic growth in China for 2015 was 7%, calculate the level of GDP in China by the end of 2015 (to the nearest $ billion). (AO1, AO2) **4 marks**

c Analyse why a country's real national income may be a poor indicator of the standard of living enjoyed by the people of that country. (AO1, AO2, AO3) **10 marks**

Aggregate demand and aggregate supply

Aggregate demand (*AD*) and aggregate supply (*AS*) are another way of modelling how the economy works. They allow us to see how their interaction leads to an equilibrium level of real national income as well as the price level at that level of output. We can see how changes in the behaviour of the different groups in the economy, such as households, will affect the equilibrium position for the economy.

⑪ Define the term 'aggregate demand'. (AO1) `3 marks`

....

....

....

⑫ Define the term 'investment'. (AO1) `3 marks`

....

....

....

⑬ Define the term 'net exports'. (AO1) `3 marks`

....

....

....

⑭ Define the term 'capital stock'. (AO1) `3 marks`

....

....

....

⑮ a From the following data, calculate the value of aggregate demand for the economy. (AO1, AO2) `4 marks`

	£m
Exports	50,230
Consumption	297,000
Imports	45,345
Investment	99,500
Government spending	125,800

....

....

....

....

....

b From the following data, calculate the value of aggregate demand for the economy. (AO1, AO2) **6 marks**

- Consumption is £345,000, of which 20% is spent on imported goods and services.
- Investment totals £99,000.
- Government expenditure totals £145,000.
- The trade balance is zero.

16 State which of the following would be a movement along the *AD* curve and which would lead to a shift in the *AD* curve. (AO1) **6 marks**

a A fall in the price level

b A rise in national income

c A rise in interest rates

d An increase in oil prices

e Greater business confidence

f A fall in wage rates

17 Decide whether the following changes would shift the aggregate demand curve to the left or to the right. (Ignore any potential effects on aggregate supply.) (AO1) **4 marks**

a A rise in income tax

b A rise in house prices

c Cuts in government expenditure

d A fall in the exchange rate

18 Decide whether the following changes would shift aggregate demand or aggregate supply. (AO1)

a   A fall in indirect taxation

....

b   A rise in income tax

....

c   A fall in the exchange rate

....

d   A rise in GDP of the UK's trading partners

....

e   A fall in commodity prices

....

f   Increased interest rates

....

19 Draw an *AD/AS* diagram to illustrate how a rise in business confidence might affect economic activity. (AO1, AO2)

20 Draw an *AD/AS* diagram to illustrate how an increase in taxation might affect economic activity. (AO1, AO2)

21 Explain two factors which would lead to an increase in investment. (AO1, AO3) `4 marks`

....

....

....

....

....

....

22 Decide whether each of the following statements is true or false. (AO1) `4 marks`

		Shift in *AD/AS*	Effect on real GDP	Effect on price level	True or false?
a	A rise in interest rates	*AD* increase	Increase	Decrease	
b	A rise in the exchange rate	*AS* decrease	Increase	Decrease	
c	Greater consumer confidence	*AD* decrease	Decrease	Increase	
d	Higher wage rates	*AS* decrease	Decrease	Increase	

23 Analyse how a reduction in interest rates can boost consumption. (AO1, AO3) `10 marks`

....

....

....

....

....

....

....

....

....

....

....

....

....

....

....

....

....

....

....

AD/AS and economic activity

How *AD* and *AS* interact is very important as this interaction and the resulting equilibrium point also affect other macroeconomic variables, such as the unemployment rate as well as the government's budget and the foreign trade balance. What factors affect the *AD/AS* curves is therefore of prime importance in managing the economy. We consider the concept of there being a short-run aggregate supply curve for determining macroeconomic equilibrium in the short term, but we also consider the idea of a long-run aggregate supply curve which determines the maximum level of output (i.e. full capacity) that can be produced by an economy.

24 **Define the term 'accelerator theory'. (AO1)** `3 marks`

25 **Define the term 'multiplier process'. (AO1)** `3 marks`

26 **Distinguish between short-run and long-run aggregate supply, giving two factors which determine each curve. (AO1, AO2)** `6 marks`

27 **If an increase in exports of £15 million and an increase in investment of £25 million combined lead to an overall increase in national income of £84 million, calculate the size of the multiplier for this economy. (AO1, AO2)** `4 marks`

28 **Draw an *AD/AS* diagram to illustrate an increase in the rate of VAT on economic activity. (AO1, AO2)** `4 marks`

29 Draw an AD/AS diagram to illustrate the effects of increased immigration into an economy and improved participation within the labour force in an economy. (AO1, AO2) `4 marks`

30 Distinguish between the following effects — by stating which of the following factors would shift short-run aggregate supply and which of them would affect long-run aggregate supply. (AO1) `5 marks`

a A fall in the exchange rate

....

b A fall in wage rates

....

c A rise in labour mobility

....

d An increase in indirect taxes

....

e Advances in technology

....

31 Explain why advances in technology might lead to increases in both aggregate supply and aggregate demand at the same time. (AO1, AO2) `4 marks`

....

....

....

....

....

....

....

....

....

....

32 'An expanded airport in London is a necessity as it will attract businesses to the UK and allow businesses to increase their output without reaching constraints on their expansion plans due to limited capacity of the capital's transport infrastructure.'

Decide whether the following statements are true or false, based on the above statement. (AO1)

5 marks

a   Greater transport capacity will lead to higher GDP due to greater investment spending by the government and private sector firms.

....

b   The long-run effect of the airport expansion will only be on aggregate demand, while aggregate supply will be unaffected.

....

c   More airport capacity increases long-run aggregate supply through a reduction in factor immobility.

....

d   Spending on airports means a larger budget deficit and this always lowers aggregate demand and leads to lower GDP.

....

e   Short-run aggregate supply will be increased due to the lower cost of flying.

....

33 Using a diagram, explain how a reduction in confidence among consumers and businesses will lead to a rise in unemployment. (AO1, AO2, AO3)

10 marks

....

....

....

....

....

....

....

....

34 Read the following extract and answer the questions that follow.

Skills shortages: holding back economic recovery

Many business leaders believe that skills shortages are appearing in many industrial sectors. This will limit future growth of these industries. Examples where shortages are include software, engineering and also in the NHS. It is believed that these shortages are so widespread that future increases in GDP will be in jeopardy unless something is done about them. Filling these gaps is not easy. It takes time and money for workers to be trained with particular skills, and steps have to be taken to ensure workers are in the right place with the right skills.

Government ministers claim that they are taking the necessary action to address these shortages. Investment in traineeships and apprenticeships has taken place, but some employers believe that they have not been allowed sufficient input into designing these courses and schemes. Others believe the government should let private businesses sort out their own training needs and instead should focus on creating adequate infrastructure to boost long-run economic growth.

a   Explain how a skills shortage will affect aggregate supply. (AO1, AO2)   `4 marks`

....

....

....

....

....

....

b   Using a diagram, show how an increase in training schemes and apprenticeships by the government can lead to higher real GDP. (AO1, AO2, AO3)   `8 marks`

....

....

....

....

....

....

c   Explain how spending on infrastructure may reduce factor immobility.
(AO1, AO2)

....

....

....

....

....

....

....

d   Analyse possible negative consequences of spending by the government on
infrastructure or training. (AO1, AO2, AO3)

....

....

....

....

....

....

....

....

....

....

....

....

....

....

....

....

....

....

....

....

....

Exam-style questions: multiple choice

Circle the letter of the answer that you think is correct.

35 The diagram shows the aggregate demand (*AD*) and aggregate supply (*AS*) curves for an economy.

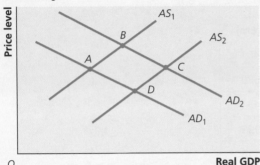

Given that *A* is the initial equilibrium position, what would be the new equilibrium position following a fall in oil prices and a reduction in wage rates?

A   Point *A*

B   Point *B*

C   Point *C*

D   Point *D*

36 Which of the following would cause a rightward shift in the aggregate demand (*AD*) curve?

A   A rise in imports

B   A rise in income tax

C   A fall in indirect tax

D   A fall in saving

37 Advances in technology in an economy are most likely to lead to:

A   Increases in long-run aggregate supply

B   Increases in short-run aggregate supply

C   A higher price level

D   Falling real GDP

38 A rise in investment caused by a rise in national income is referred to as:

A   The multiplier

B   The accelerator

C   Inflation

D   Capital stock

39 An increase in interest rates is most likely to have the following effect:

A   Lower rates of saving

B   Higher consumption

C   Lower exchange rate

D   Reduced inflationary pressure

Exam-style questions: data response

40 **Read Extracts A and B and answer the following questions.**

Extract A

The following table relates to the UK economy between 2005 and 2014.

Year	Household consumption (£m)	GDP (£m)
2005	973,088	1,549,491
2006	994,192	1,596,628
2007	1,021,686	1,637,432
2008	1,016,522	1,631,995
2009	982,485	1,561,646
2010	986,956	1,591,494
2011	985,843	1,617,677
2012	1,000,859	1,628,338
2013	1,018,246	1,655,447
2014	1,044,378	1,704,998

Extract B

Households, normally the driving force of any economic recovery, have been reluctant to commit themselves to their normal spending booms. In the UK, consumption is the largest component of aggregate demand by a long way. However, interest rates remained at a record low of 0.5% for over 6 years and have not encouraged a return to the spending ways of the typical UK household.

Economists suggest that the reluctance comes from a patchy economic recovery which has seen confidence returning very slowly. Taxes have been increased on households and welfare spending cut. The government believes consumers' confidence will return, especially with unemployment in the UK falling faster than expected. However, others are not so sure, as many of the jobs created after the 2008–09 recession have been either part time or temporary, which does not normally equate with strong rises in confidence.

a **Define the term 'consumption'.** 3 marks

b **Using Extract A, calculate consumption as a percentage of UK GDP in 2014.** 4 marks

c Using Extract A, identify two significant points of comparison between UK real GDP and consumption over the period shown. **4 marks**

d Explain two uses that a government can make of GDP data. **4 marks**

e Explain how economic growth may fall, even with very low interest rates. **10 marks**

f To what extent might cuts in interest rates boost UK consumption?

25 marks

Topic 3

Economic performance

Economic growth and the economic cycle

In the long run, the economy's growth will be limited by the growth over time in the productive potential of the economy — the maximum amount of output that can be produced. However, in the short run, the rate of economic growth will vary. This variation of short-run growth from the long-term rate of growth — otherwise known as the trend growth — gives us the economic cycle.

Each stage of this repeated pattern observed within the economic cycle will lead to different results for each economic indicator of the government's economic objectives. The deviation of short-run growth from long-run trend growth gives us output gaps (both positive and negative) in the economy.

Economic shocks will also occur which could have a supply-side or a demand-side cause. These can have unexpected positive or negative consequences for the macroeconomy.

---

1 Define the term 'trend growth'. (AO1)　　`3 marks`

....

....

....

2 State three features of an economic recovery. (AO1)　　`3 marks`

....

....

....

3 Distinguish between a demand-side shock and a supply-side shock. Comment on whether you think these can be equally problematic for an economy. (AO1, AO2, AO3)　`6 marks`

....

....

....

....

....

....

....

....

....

4 Which of the following would be seen as characteristics of an economic downturn? (AO1) **3 marks**

   a Falling inflation

   b Falling unemployment

   c Increased trade deficit

   d Increased budget deficit

   e Slower growth in GDP

5 Using an *AD/AS* diagram, explain the economic effects on the UK of a supply-side shock caused by a sudden large increase in the price of oil. (AO1, AO2, AO3) **10 marks**

Employment and unemployment

Unemployment refers to those looking for work who cannot find employment. Minimising unemployment is a key objective of the government. However, to minimise unemployment it is important to understand that there are various causes of unemployment in an economy — these include cyclical, frictional and structural causes of unemployment. These types of unemployment can also be categorised as those caused by demand-side factors and those caused by supply-side factors.

6 Define the term 'full employment'. (AO1)   `3 marks`

....

....

7 Define the term 'structural unemployment'. (AO1)   `3 marks`

....

....

8 Define the term 'cyclical unemployment'. (AO1)   `3 marks`

....

....

....

9 Briefly distinguish between demand-side and supply-side causes of unemployment. Why do you think this distinction is of interest to the government? (AO1, AO2)   `5 marks`

....

....

....

....

....

....

....

10 'People are either unemployed or employed.' Explain two ways in which this statement is inaccurate. (AO1, AO2)   `4 marks`

....

....

....

....

....

11 Explain two ways in which structural unemployment can occur. (AO1, AO2)   `4 marks`

....

....

....

....

....

....

12 'The solution to high unemployment is easy — the government must simply spend more on new roads, new train lines and our armed forces.'

Analyse why the above statement does not provide an adequate solution to high unemployment. (AO1, AO2, AO3)

10 marks

....

....

....

....

....

....

....

....

....

....

....

....

....

....

13 Draw an *AD/AS* diagram to illustrate the effect of a rise in the level of cyclical unemployment on economic activity. (AO1, AO2)

4 marks

Inflation

Inflation refers to a rise in the average level of general prices. Achieving stable prices is another key economic objective. If a government is to manage the level of inflation and keep it at the level it desires then it is important to understand what causes inflation.

Inflation has two main causes: demand-pull and cost-push. We also need to understand that commodity price changes as well as changes in the global external environment can have a significant effect on the inflation rate.

14 Define the term 'inflation'. (AO1) 3 marks

....

....

....

15 Define the term 'disinflation'. (AO1) 3 marks

....

....

....

16 Define the term 'deflation'. (AO1) 3 marks

....

....

....

17 Categorise the following occurrences into whether they will contribute inflationary or deflationary pressures to an economy: (AO1) 6 marks

   a A fall in the exchange rate

   b High unemployment

   c A sustained rise in business and consumer confidence

   d Increased pressure by trade unions to improve worker conditions

   e Lower interest rates for a prolonged period

   f Sharp drops in oil prices

....

....

....

....

....

....

18 Draw an *AD/AS* diagram to illustrate cost-push inflation. (AO1, AO2) 4 marks

19 Draw an *AD/AS* diagram to illustrate the effects of a reduction in demand-pull inflation on economic activity. (AO1, AO2) `4 marks`

The balance of payments

The balance of payments records all the financial transactions between the UK and the rest of the world. The current account of the balance of payments focuses on short-term transfers of money arising from the trade of goods and services (exports and imports), as well as income generated from factors of production located outside the country of ownership. The government is aiming for balance on the current account, so it will be looking at how to reduce the level of imports and how to boost the level of exports.

20 Define the term 'primary income'. (AO1) `3 marks`

21 Define the term 'current account deficit'. (AO1) `3 marks`

22 Define the term 'secondary income'. (AO1) `3 marks`

23 Explain why, although the balance of payments should have a zero balance, the current account can sometimes reach incredibly large deficits. (AO1, AO2) `4 marks`

24 Draw an *AD/AS* diagram to illustrate the impact of a rise in inflation in the UK relative to inflation in the economies of our close trading partners. (AO1, AO2)   `4 marks`

25 From the following data for an economy, calculate the current account balance (assuming the balances relate to surpluses unless otherwise stated). (AO1, AO2)   `4 marks`

	£ million
Balance on goods deficit	33,121
Balance on services	27,414
Primary income balance	11,094
Secondary income deficit	4,376

....

....

26 The following data relate to the UK balance of payments for 2014.

	£ million
Exports of goods	292,204
Imports of goods	413,419
Exports of services	215,020
Imports of services	129,029
Primary income deficit	44,976

a Based on these data, calculate the trade balance for the UK in 2014. (AO1, AO2)   `4 marks`

....

....

b In 2014, the secondary income balance was in deficit at £25,451 million. Calculate the overall current account balance for 2014. (AO1, AO2)   `4 marks`

....

....

....

....

c   Explain how continued recovery of economic growth in the EU economies would be good for the UK's current account balance. (AO1, AO2)   `4 marks`

....

....

....

....

....

27 Explain two factors that would lead to an increase in UK imports. (AO1, AO2)   `4 marks`

....

....

....

....

....

28 Explain the effects of a fall in the exchange rate on the current account of a country's balance of payments. (AO1, AO2, AO3)   `10 marks`

....

....

....

....

....

....

....

....

....

....

....

....

....

....

....

....

....

Policy conflicts

Output gaps are considered in terms of their impact on the macroeconomic objectives of inflation and unemployment.

The policy conflicts that may exist within an economy (in the short run, at least) may be solved through the use of different policies for each macroeconomic objective.

29 Define the term 'output gap'. (AO1)　　　　　　　　　**3 marks**

....

....

30 Explain, giving an example, the term 'policy conflict'. (AO1, AO2)　　　**4 marks**

....

....

....

....

31 Explain how the use of different policies can resolve the policy conflict that exists between achieving economic growth and the increasing deficit on the current account of the balance of payments. (AO1, AO2)　　　**4 marks**

....

....

....

....

....

32 Which two of the following describe a policy conflict that could face the UK economy? (AO1)　　　**2 marks**

a　The falling budget deficit that accompanies rising GDP

b　The rise in inflation that comes as a result of rapid economic growth

c　The rising incomes of rich households relative to those of poorer households

d　The fall in the current account deficit that often comes from a recession

....

33 Using *AD/AS* diagrams, show how a policy conflict between unemployment and inflation may exist, and how in the long run this policy conflict may not exist. (AO1, AO2, AO3)　　**15 marks**

34 Read the following extract and answer the questions that follow.

A different kind of recession

The financial crisis which led to the recession of 2008 was largely unexpected a few years earlier. Most recessions in the UK have occurred due to the effect of high interest rates needed to bring down the rate of inflation. This time it was different. Interest rates since the late 1990s have rarely been above 5% — a far cry from the double-digit interest rates that were the norm throughout the 1980s and early 1990s. However, even with modest interest rates, the recession which followed was deep.

The following chart shows the quarterly change in economic growth in the UK from 2004 to the start of 2015.

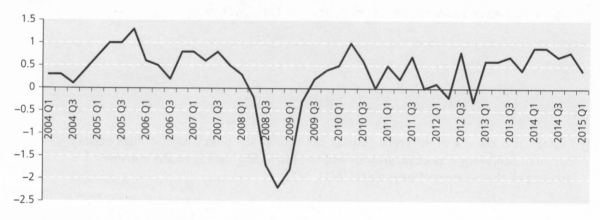

Economic growth (% change on previous quarter)

a In which quarter was economic growth: (AO1)   3 marks

   i Highest?

   ....

   ii Lowest?

   ....

b How long did the recession last that started in 2008? (AO1)   1 mark

   ....

c The financial crisis of 2007–08 can be described as an 'economic shock'.
   Explain what this term means. (AO1)   3 marks

   ....

   ....

d Explain three characteristics of a recession. (AO1, AO2)   9 marks

   ....

   ....

   ....

   ....

   ....

   ....

   ....

e **Discuss whether there will be any policy conflicts in the government's attempt to end a recession. (AO1, AO2, AO3)** `25 marks`

Exam-style questions: multiple choice

Circle the letter of the answer that you think is correct.

35 This table shows a summary of the balance of payments on current account for an economy in 2015.

	£m
Exports of goods	128
Exports of services	45
Imports of goods	134
Imports of services	41
Net primary income	−18
Net secondary income	−5

The balance on the current account of the balance of payments would be:

1 mark

A +£20 million

B −£20 million

C −£25 million

D −£2 million

36 An economy is currently experiencing a positive output gap. In the short run the economy is most likely to experience:

1 mark

A An increase in inflation

B An increase in unemployment

C An increased budget deficit

D An increase in trend growth

37 Which of the following is most likely to reduce the UK's current account deficit?

1 mark

A A fall in the amount of foreign currency needed to purchase sterling

B A rise in UK GDP

C A rise in inflation in the UK relative to overseas inflation

D A rise in UK consumer spending

38 It is observed that in an economy during the recession phase of the economic cycle there is likely to be a rise in:

1 mark

A Investment

B Consumption

C Unemployment

D Inflation

39 Which of the following is most likely to lead to inflation?

1 mark

A Increased aggregate demand at full employment

B A rise in the exchange rate

C A rise in unemployment

D Lower indirect taxation

Exam-style questions: data response

40 **Read Extracts A and B and answer the following questions.** **Total: 50 marks**

Extract A

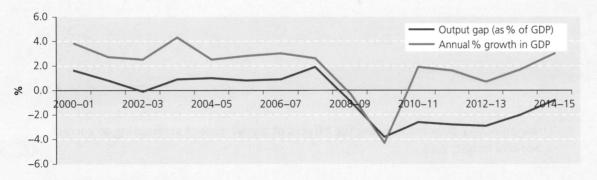

UK economic growth and the output gap

Extract B

In 2013, the UK economy reached its previous peak level of GDP that it had reached in 2008. This represents, some would argue, 5 years of lost growth that can never be recaptured. Others would argue that the slow growth of the long recovery is the price that has to be paid for the boom years leading up to the 2008–09 recession. Chancellors of the exchequer might believe they have eliminated the economic cycle — put an end to 'boom and bust' — through skilful management of the economy. However, the recession and the recovery seem to suggest that the economic cycle is alive and well. Some are already worrying about the next boom — with rising house prices being an early indicator of stronger growth conditions.

a   **State what stage of the economic cycle the UK economy was in during:**

 i   **2008–09** **1 mark**

....

 ii   **2010–11** **1 mark**

....

 iii **2003–04** **1 mark**

....

b   **Define the term 'negative output gap'.** **4 marks**

....

....

....

....

c   **Using Extract A, identify two significant points of comparison between UK economic growth and the size of the output gap over the period shown.** **4 marks**

....

....

....

....

d Explain why the output gap decreases in size after 2009.

e Draw an *AD/AS* diagram showing the effects of a government attempting to correct a positive output gap.

f Explain three features of the boom stage of the economic cycle.

g **To what extent should a government always take action to ensure there are no booms in the economy?**

25 marks

Topic 4

Macroeconomic policy

Monetary policy

Monetary policy refers to changes in the price of money (the interest rate), the money supply and the availability of credit. Changes in monetary policy affect the macroeconomic indicators. Interest rates are used in the UK mainly to manage the level of inflation and also economic growth as a secondary objective.

Changes in interest rates are decided monthly by the Monetary Policy Committee (MPC) of the Bank of England. These changes not only affect growth (and employment) and inflation, but also affect the exchange rate which will indirectly affect other parts of the economy.

1 Define the term 'monetary policy'. (AO1)　　　　　　　　　　　`3 marks`

....

2 Define the term 'contractionary monetary policy'. (AO1)　　　`3 marks`

....

3 Briefly state three likely effects of a rise in interest rates. (AO1)　`3 marks`

....

....

4 The MPC will increase interest rates if it thinks inflation is likely to rise above its target range in the medium term. Other than just 'rising prices', state three factors that would make the MPC more likely to raise interest rates in the near future. Provide a brief explanation of why you think these factors may increase future inflation. (AO1, AO2, AO3)　　`9 marks`

....

....

....

....

....

....

....

....

5 Describe two ways in which a change in the exchange rate will affect macroeconomic performance. (AO1, AO2)   4 marks

....

....

....

....

6 Draw an *AD/AS* diagram to illustrate the effects of higher interest rates on economic activity. (AO1, AO2)   4 marks

7 Explain how a rise in interest rates can lead to a reduction in inflation. (AO1, AO2, AO3)   10 marks

....

....

....

....

....

....

....

....

....

....

....

....

....

....

....

....

....

....

Fiscal policy

Changes in taxation and government expenditure form the government's fiscal policy. Changes in fiscal policy will have effects on the various macroeconomic indicators that the government is attempting to influence in achieving its objectives.

Taxes can be levied in the economy in a number of different ways. How these taxes are used and what level they are will impact on the ability of the government to achieve its economic objectives. Changes in fiscal policy can also be used as part of the government's supply-side policy.

8 Define the term 'direct tax'. (AO1) `3 marks`

9 Define the term 'fiscal policy'. (AO1) `3 marks`

10 State three examples of incomes that are taxed in the UK. (AO1) `3 marks`

11 Distinguish between regressive and progressive taxes — give an example of each in the UK. (AO1, AO2) `4 marks`

12 Describe how changes in tax can affect *both* aggregate demand and aggregate supply. (AO1, AO2) `4 marks`

13 Explain two ways in which a government can reduce a budget deficit. (AO1, AO2) `4 marks`

14 Distinguish between the national debt and the budget balance. (AO1, AO2)   `4 marks`

15 Some would argue that VAT on petrol is a regressive tax, while others would argue that it is a proportional tax. Explain how both views might be correct. (AO1, AO2)   `5 marks`

16 Outline three ways in which higher taxes may reduce economic activity in an economy. (AO1, AO2, AO3)   `9 marks`

17 Explain one microeconomic effect and one macroeconomic effect of higher taxes. (AO1, AO2)   `4 marks`

18 The following table summarises the different tax bands for incomes earned in the UK for the 2015/16 financial year.

Tax rate	Income range
Tax-free allowance:	£0–£10,600
Basic rate of 20%:	£10,600–£42,385
Higher rate of 40%:	£42,385+
Additional rate of 45%:	£150,000+

Calculate the amounts of income tax paid by those who earn the following amounts:

a £15,000 (AO1, AO2) `3 marks`

b £30,000 (AO1, AO2) `4 marks`

c £50,000 (AO1, AO2) `4 marks`

19 Draw an *AD/AS* diagram to illustrate the effects of higher rates of indirect taxes on economic activity. (AO1, AO2) `4 marks`

20 Explain two features of using a progressive system of tax for incomes. (AO1, AO2) `4 marks`

Supply-side policy

Long-run growth comes from increases in the productive capacity of the economy. This is shown by rightward shifts in the *LRAS* curve. This is referred to as the supply side of the economy. Improvements to this supply side can come from general supply-side improvements or specific supply-side policies.

Supply-side policies are implemented by the government to increase the long-run growth rate of the economy. They will also affect the level of unemployment, the level of inflation and the foreign trade balance.

21 **Define the term 'privatisation'. (AO1)** `3 marks`

22 **Define the term 'deregulation'. (AO1)** `3 marks`

23 **Explain the term 'labour market flexibility' and give an example of this as used in the UK. (AO1)** `3 marks`

24 **Distinguish between 'supply-side policies' and 'supply-side improvements'. (AO1)** `3 marks`

25 **The following are limitations of economic policy. Categorise these according to the policy (monetary, fiscal or supply-side) that they are a critique of: (AO1, AO2)** `6 marks`

a   A higher national debt will potentially increase future interest rates.

b   Those less well-off often find their incomes reduced even if they keep their jobs.

c   Savers are often penalised by this policy.

d   Governments have not always found competition is vigorous enough in the industries they have targeted.

e   Working hours often cannot be changed in response to changes in tax rates.

f   Once they have been cut so far, they cannot be cut further even if more stimulus is needed.

26 Draw an *AD/AS* diagram to illustrate the effects of a successful programme of trade union reform on economic activity. (AO1, AO2) `4 marks`

27 In each case, give a brief explanation of how the following will increase the long-run aggregate supply of an economy. (AO1, AO2, AO3) `12 marks`

   a Spending on education and training

   b Income tax cuts

   c Welfare reform

   d Industrial policy

28 Although cuts in income tax are seen as an effective supply-side policy, governments have been reluctant to cut income tax in recent years. State and explain two reasons why this may be the case. (AO1, AO2) `4 marks`

29 The following list contains statements of economic policy. Categorise these into monetary, fiscal and supply-side policies. (AO1) **6 marks**

a Encouraging consumption with lower costs of borrowing

b Selling off nationalised industries for contributions to government revenue

c Quantitative easing

d Increasing the requirements needed to claim unemployment benefit

e Reductions in government subsidies to all businesses to reduce the budget deficit

f Grants given to businesses to boost the economy in local regions in the UK

....

....

....

....

....

....

30 Read this extract and answer the questions that follow.

Time for interest rates to rise?

After 6 years of interest rates at 0.5%, some economists raised the issue of whether it was time in 2015 for interest rates to be increased. The 0.5% rate reached in 2009 was meant to provide a monetary stimulus at the time of the financial crisis. No one realistically expected this 'emergency' low rate to prevail so long.

Others felt that interest rates should be left at this low level given the austerity plans and the UK government's tight fiscal position. With cuts in government expenditure promised in both the 2010 coalition government and the proceeding 2015 Conservative majority government likely to hit consumer confidence, it was seen as an appropriate policy response to keep interest rates low while fiscal policy was very tight.

Inflation, rather unexpectedly, remained low from 2013 onwards and even briefly dipped into deflationary territory in 2015. Given the ongoing 2% target for inflation and the most likely path being an undershoot of this target in 2015, it seemed unlikely that interest rates were going to be raised much before 2016.

a Explain the following terms used in the above passage:

i 'Monetary stimulus' (AO1) **3 marks**

....

....

....

ii 'Tight fiscal position' (AO1) **3 marks**

....

....

....

b Explain why low interest rates were seen as an 'appropriate policy response' despite the economic recovery since 2009. (AO1, AO2)

6 marks

....

....

....

....

....

....

c Explain two reasons why the government might want to keep fiscal policy 'very tight'. (AO1, AO2)

6 marks

....

....

....

....

....

....

d Using an *AD/AS* diagram, analyse the effects of an interest rate rise in 2016 on macroeconomic performance. (AO1, AO2, AO3)

10 marks

....

....

....

....

....

....

....

....

Exam-style questions: multiple choice

Circle the letter of the answer that you think is correct.

31 A policy of higher interest rates is most likely to lead to which combination of outcomes?

`1 mark`

	Inflation	Unemployment	Exchange rate	Economic growth
A	Decrease	Decrease	Increase	Increase
B	Decrease	Increase	Increase	Decrease
C	Increase	Decrease	Decrease	Increase
D	Increase	Increase	Decrease	Decrease

32 An economy experiences both persistent deficits on the current account and high unemployment. Which policy is most likely to lead to a reduced current account deficit and lower unemployment?

`1 mark`

A Cuts in direct taxation

B A fall in the exchange rate

C Higher government spending

D Higher interest rates

33 In which situation would contractionary fiscal policy be the most appropriate policy? `1 mark`

A Increased budget surplus

B Negative output gap growing

C Rising current account surplus

D Inflationary pressure emerging

34 Which of the following is an example of a supply-side policy? `1 mark`

A Reducing welfare benefits

B Rise in entrepreneurial spirit in economy

C Cutting indirect taxes

D Nationalisation of monopolies

35 Unemployment is rising quickly in an economy. Which combination of policies is most likely to reduce the rate of unemployment?

`1 mark`

	Interest rates	Government spending	Taxation
A	Higher	Lower	Higher
B	Lower	Lower	Higher
C	Higher	Higher	Lower
D	Lower	Higher	Lower

Exam-style questions: data response

36 Read Extracts A, B and C and answer the following questions.

Extract A

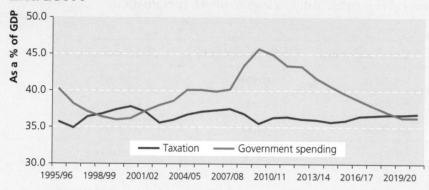

Source: OBR

UK government expenditure and taxation, 1995–2021 (2015/16 onwards are forecast data)

Extract B

Economists have been surprised about how far unemployment has fallen since the end of the 2008–09 recession. Even the Bank of England did not expect unemployment to fall this quickly. Government officials believe the surprising fall is due to the success of a range of supply-side policies implemented over recent years. Making it easier for firms to take on workers has helped. Creating more incentives to make work attractive has also helped. The large rise in the tax-free allowance all workers can benefit from has certainly made a difference. Those working full time on the minimum wage now pay only a small amount of income tax.

Extract C

Critics of the government's welfare reforms point out that the reduction in benefits designed to encourage people into work has led to significant increases in poverty. The rise in VAT in 2011 and the imposition of the 'bedroom' tax, as well as the benefit cap, have all made it harder for those on low or no incomes. Critics also point to the fact that many jobs that have been created are part time or temporary — not what people really want.

a   **Define the term 'budget surplus'.**

....

....

....

b   **Using Extract A, identify two significant points of comparison between UK government expenditure and taxation over the period shown.**

....

....

....

....

....

....

....

c In the financial year 2020/21, UK GDP is forecast to be £2,326 billion. If government expenditure is forecast to be 36.3% of GDP, calculate the actual forecast level of government expenditure in £.

`4 marks`

....

....

d Draw an *AD/AS* diagram to illustrate the impact of the government implementing a range of supply-side policies.

`4 marks`

e Analyse the effects of higher taxes on economic performance.

`10 marks`

....

....

....

....

....

....

....

....

....

....

f Discuss whether the government's supply-side policy can be seen as a success.

`25 marks`

....

....

....

....

....

....

....

....

(Answer lines continue on p. 56)

Philip Allan, an imprint of Hodder Education, an Hachette UK company,
Blenheim Court, George Street, Banbury, Oxfordshire OX16 5BH

Orders

Bookpoint Ltd, 130 Park Drive, Milton Park, Abingdon, Oxfordshire
OX14 4SB

tel: 01235 827827

fax: 01235 400401

e-mail: education@bookpoint.co.uk

Lines are open 9.00 a.m.–5.00 p.m., Monday to Saturday, with a
24-hour message answering service.

You can also order through the Hodder Education website:
www.hoddereducation.co.uk

© David Horner and Steve Stoddard 2016

ISBN 978-1-4718-4456-0

First printed 2016

Impression number   5   4   3

Year   2020   2019

This guide has been written specifically to support students preparing for
the AQA AS and A-level Economics examinations. The content has been
neither approved nor endorsed by AQA and remains the sole responsibility
of the authors.

Typeset by Integra Software Services Pvt. Ltd., Pondicherry, India

Printed in Dubai

Hachette UK's policy is to use papers that are natural, renewable and
recyclable products and made from wood grown in sustainable forests.
The logging and manufacturing processes are expected to conform to the
environmental regulations of the country of origin.

ISBN 978-1-4718-4456-0

6 Explain the difference between an increase in national income and an increase in economic growth. (AO1) `3 marks`

....

....

....

....

7 Explain how a rise in incomes among the poorest 10% of households can still be accompanied by rising inequality across the economy. (AO1) `3 marks`

....

....

....

....

8 Distinguish between macroeconomic objectives and macroeconomic policies. (AO1) `3 marks`

....

....

....

....

9 At the year-end, GDP in an economy was valued at £1,378,000 million. Over the next year, the economy experienced economic growth of 2.2%. What would be the value of GDP by the end of this year? (AO1, AO2) `4 marks`

....

....

....

....

....

10 After economic growth of 1.5%, an economy's GDP reached a level of $980 billion. Calculate the value of GDP before the growth occurred. (AO1, AO2) `4 marks`

....

....

....

....

11 GDP at the end of year 1 was valued at £456,000 million. If economic growth in year 2 was 2.8%, calculate the level of GDP by the end of year 2. (AO1, AO2) `4 marks`

....

....

....

....

....

Topic 1

The measurement of economic performance

Macroeconomic objectives

The government has a number of goals — objectives — that it wishes to achieve for the economy. These include:

- achieving economic growth
- minimising unemployment
- achieving stable prices
- balancing the budget on the government's finances
- achieving balance on foreign trade

Sometimes, there will be a policy conflict which means achieving one objective moves the government further away from achieving its other objectives. However, some would argue that these policy conflicts only exist in the short run and that in the long run it might be possible to achieve (or move closer to achieving) all objectives simultaneously. There are even some economists who would argue that these conflicts do not exist even in the short run.

---

1 **Define the term 'economic growth'. (AO1)**   `3 marks`

....

2 **Define the term 'distribution of income'. (AO1)**   `3 marks`

....

3 **Define the term 'balance of payments'. (AO1)**   `3 marks`

....

4 **Define the term 'price stability'. (AO1)**   `3 marks`

....

....

5 **The balance on the government's budget would involve looking at which two of the following economic variables? (AO1)**   `2 marks`

   a **Exports**

   b **Government expenditure**

   c **Taxation**

   d **Imports**

....

....

3

Contents

① This workbook will help you to prepare for the Paper 2 AS/Year 1 A-level (The national economy in a global context) exam.

② Your exam is 1 hour 30 minutes long and includes a range of questions. The exam is divided into two sections. In Section A you will answer 20 multiple-choice questions worth 20 marks. In Section B you will answer one data-response question from a choice of two worth 50 marks — both covering the national economy in a global context. Short- and long-answer questions need planning — this workbook will help.

③ This workbook is divided into four topics. For each topic there are:

- stimulus materials, including key terms and short explanations of concepts
- short-answer questions that build up to exam-style questions
- spaces for you to write or plan your answers
- questions which test your mathematical skills

④ Answering the questions will help you to build your skills and meet the assessment objectives: AO1 (knowledge and understanding), AO2 (application), AO3 (analysis) and AO4 (evaluation).

⑤ You still need to read your textbook and refer to your revision guides and lesson notes.

⑥ Marks available are indicated for all questions so that you can gauge the level of detail required in your answers.

⑦ Timings are given for the exam-style questions to make your practice as realistic as possible.

⑧ Answers are available at:
www.hoddereducation.co.uk/workbookanswers

AQA

AS/A LEVEL

WORKBOOK

Economics

Section 2: The national economy in a global context

David Horner and Steve Stoddard

HODDER
EDUCATION
LEARN MORE